FALLING OFF THE MOON

POEMS OF TRANSFORMATION

DEVAVANI LAWRENCE

CREATIVE SPIRIT PRESS

Cover by Andrea Reider Design, www.ReiderBooks.com

Book layout by Beth Barany, Barany Consulting, www.BethBarany.com

❀ Created with Vellum

For my desert sister, Sher,
Who knows my journey by heart.

CONTENTS

Rise up nimbly and
go on your strange journey
to the ocean of meanings.
The stream knows it can't stay
on the mountain.

Leave and don't look away from
the sun as you go, in whose light
you are sometimes crescent,
sometimes full.

~ *Jalal al-Din Rumi*

GUESTHOUSE

Two years into living on an island and seven months into a global pandemic, I gave birth to a new self. Quietly, and coming out of a long strange fog of death dreams and fear, I woke up much like Dante. In the middle of the night, in the middle of my life... I awoke to find myself in a dark wood.

Surrounded by old fears and familiar patterns of resistance, suddenly I died. I stopped thinking in all my usual ways. Stopped doing, stopped caring even. Stopped throwing myself into activity or acts of caregiving. Just stopped in the way that death stops even the most vital among us.

In stopping, I became still. Literally, all I could do was breathe. In and out, breathing and not speaking. I had no words. Present only to intense emotion, I lay still and eventually slept. When I awoke, I was changed. The best way I can describe this sensation of change was that the pattern of my days had become disrupted. I no longer moved in my usual ways. My motivation for doing routine tasks shifted. My center of gravity was recalibrating. I wasn't walking a worn path, wanting the same old steady comforting habits of doing. My desires followed a new trajectory. Now I wanted the new life I had been dreaming about but resisting. The good habits I hoped for but didn't practice. Suddenly, I was *all in*. How was this possible?

I believe that in each of us live many aspects of self. And each aspect of self has her own name, her own voice. During the many seasons of a human life, these diverse voices express in response to the season being lived. The strongest, most urgent voice usually presides. But sometimes during times of transformation, the aspect previously in charge may be unwilling to give up her seat to another. A subconscious struggle ensues which may manifest as emotional or physical crisis. In the vehicle of our forward movement, we suddenly experience a change of drivers, and fear whispers in our ear that we are dying.

In my case, for months my sleep was punctuated by death dreams, accompanied by a strange nightly numbness in my feet and thoughts about dying. I became worn out with night after night of restlessness and fear, accompanied by physical symptoms which were quite frankly alarming and for which I had no explanation. I considered writing my will just in case the death dreams were messages from beyond to get ready to go.

Exhausted by it all, one day I just had enough and decided to finally turn and face the thing chasing me. Face my own death. Stare it in the eye and stop running scared. I initiated my checklist: Go to a doctor for help. Be accountable for my circumstances and my choices. Start moving my body. Push through my reluctance to change.

Henry David Thoreau wrote that when we take one step toward our dreams, the whole universe takes ten steps toward us. When I took one step toward my truth, the universe said *Yes* and began nudging my heart and world back to center – closer to my source and a more loving and lifegiving awareness. That divine *Yes* returned me to my wholeness – my ground of being that fear had tried to shut down and numb out.

In the 13th century Rumi wrote, *"This being human is a guesthouse, every day a new arrival."*

Saying yes to life is not only a daily practice, but one which continues to remind me that I am not in charge, just responsible for getting out of my own way in order to welcome the divine arrival of the guest.

Today, my death dreams are a thing of the past. My health has rebounded, and I have returned at last to the creative life I love so much. I am composing, singing and writing again with a newfound delight. This book, which has waited so many years for me to create, comes at a time in our collective history when many of us are moving through tremendous heart-wrenching change. My hope is that something I have written will ring the bell of truth for someone else and inspire their inevitable life transitions to flow with greater ease and grace, welcoming new life into their own divinely human guesthouse.

Devavani
November 2022

THE POEMS

Reading or writing poetry has provided the water of inspiration for me in times of personal drought, offering a refuge for the voice of my spiritual longing. Whenever I felt words pressing from within, or coming from above, I did my best to capture them by writing what I heard. For me, poetry artfully and clearly delivers the full circumference of human experience in all its complexity and bestows the gift of beauty in return for truth.

In this collection spanning many years, my poems resemble children from the same family. The poems are personal, as each one carries some part of my evolution as a woman moving through years of chaos, challenge and change. I wrote them in moments of grief or revelation, trusting that my feet were on the right path.

Someone once said that if we really knew the breakdown a seed must undergo in order to grow, we wouldn't use it as our metaphor for living. But like the growth cycle of that seed, my poetry also speaks to stages of undoing, death and resurrection, growth and connection – themes that are understood gradually in the way rainwater will reveal roots in the earth.

More importantly, my poems are testimony to the unraveling,

unfolding, messy beautiful living that many of us navigate in return for liberation. Themes of freedom and wholeness seem to seep into everything I want to say. Knowing that the true nature of wholeness arises from radical inclusion, my wish is that my poems might lift the veil which hides the dark side of the moon, as well as share her illuminating light.

If with this small offering, I can assemble my various parts like the Tin Man did in *Wizard of Oz*, I will be content for the heart it holds. The freedom to express authentically as myself is the jewel beyond price.

Devavani,
November 2022

NIGHT SKY

I HAD TO BE OUTSIDE TONIGHT FOR
the stars were holding the high watch,
sending messages across millennia as
dreams falling to earth in images.

A black hat on my head and
my hair tucked up into it neatly,
I was a twirler like Rumi.
I whirled for God, my
skirts flying around and around until
all else faded and there was only the one
clear center.

And Rumi, unmistakable in any language,
spoke to me across centuries.
Reminding me that he too
watched the night sky, and
was a stargazer in conversation with
points of light,
reciting poetry so radiant,
the dome of heaven was lit with its meaning...

That the Infinite One makes its home
in the human heart,
that we live forever and are loved beyond words.

WHAT IF...

WHAT IF THIS MORNING SUN SHINING UPON MY
FACE WAS RISEN TODAY JUST FOR ME?

What if this stillness was the whole world paused in its
orbit waiting for my smile to dawn slowly?

What if this breeze blown over miles of deep ocean,
singing and breathing, had traveled from distant lands
for the sole purpose of caressing my cheek gently in
this moment now?

What if God in her heaven, resting and reading, put down
her book as I entered and smiled at me, her eyes saying
how her heart filled to bursting in my presence?

What if all of life was created as perfectly as a newborn
just so I could feel free to dance and sing in it? So the
soft animal of my body could love what it loves and
my soul revel in joy?

What if this light, this breath, this look, this life were
    meeting me here in this moment, keeping a promise
    made to me when the earth was fresh and new,
    keeping it in this appointed hour saying,

"Yes... YES,
You are alive,
You are here,
You have arrived and
You are free,
My Beloved,
Most Holy."

ON BEING A WOMAN

IT'S NOT SURPRISING FOR A WOMAN TO GO
UNDERGROUND.

She can't live out in the open forever, onstage or in the
limelight open to all eyes and every public opinion.

No, a woman must dig down into herself in certain
seasons of life to discover what lives there in the
silence and curate that for her soul's delight.

A woman must go away at times to travel and to be alone.
To stop her doingness in order to nurture her being-
ness. A woman must dream and search the sky for her
own truth. She must feel and divine the fuse that fuels
the flower's bloom.

A woman must dwell in the long tones of her own voice.

A woman must stop and stop and stop again to survey her
own landscape and map her way forward. She must
walk to the secret cliff where bees drip their honey-
comb from ancient limestone crags and wild pigs root
under the massive tree canopy at midnight.

A woman must breathe and sigh and empty. Then pause
to dream some more before moving to give life to her
visions with words, colors, shapes, music and sound.

She must scan the horizon of her own soul, following
music that only she can hear in order to hold sacred
the one clear pebble of truth she finds there.

ON LEAVING

I LEFT THE HORSE LIFE, THE CHURCH LIFE, THE
TEACHING LIFE, THE MARRIED LIFE.

Left home, left my town, my country, community and
friends.

Pulled up roots gently.

Walked away from the familiar, the beloved, the history of
my past. From childhood haunts, from people, places
and things. From trainings and degrees, performance
stages, classrooms and houses.

Freed myself of expectation and predictability, watched as
layers of conditioning and tradition slowly dissolved.

Dropped the burden of my responsibility to others to
answer the whispered sighs of my own heart asking,
"If not now, then when?"

Answered with gratitude and goodbyes. Farewell desert
mountains, soft California beaches. Farewell my
friends... until we meet again.

Nothing is wrong. I love you.

I gazed ahead into a future world still forming and felt her
breathing. Closed my eyes to see new life beckoning.

Heard the gentle shush of unseen waves moving toward
me while invisible breezes unlatched ancient doors.

Followed their secret sounds until Time chose my
moment... and I

Leapt.

I AM THE ONE

I AM THE ONE WHO WALKED AWAY.

I am the one who sleeps alone.
I am the one who has a voice, who is looking out her eyes
in a new way.
I am the one who is stretching her wings, praying a new
prayer and singing a new song.

I am the one who is digging deeper and weeping over the
bones found there.
I am the one who is ancient and innocent at the same
time.
I am the one who aches to love and be loved, who longs
for connection.
But I am the one who guards her freedom and wraps
aloneness like a precious soul blanket around her
body.

I am mother, wife, sister, daughter and friend for life.
I am the one who thought that's what Love does:
  Give All.
I gave all, not counting myself worthy of my own giving.
I am the one who discovered she could fly mid-fall, step-
  ping off the cliff into emptiness.

I am the one who chose a new possibility and thought a
  new thought.
I am the one who seeks and feels the silent place where
  God enters in Stillness.

I am the one who knows my mind cannot carry me where
  I need to go - I need wings for that.
I am the one who bows down to the holy sacred miracle
  of my body and is grateful, grateful for my life.

WAITING

WHILE YOU QUIETLY REARRANGED THE ROOMS OF
   YOUR HEART,
I stood waiting outside your door,
my arms full of flowers.

Sensing the coming shadows
you stepped in front of your tender heart,
moving to protect for all the usual reasons.
Not remembering that sunlight cannot warm
where it isn't felt.
Nor realizing that the truest voice in you just
fled deeper into hiding.

But here... here in the house of your belonging,
doors and windows open as if by magic.
Breezes dance through and the luminous roundness of
moonlight rises above a darkening world.

Remember...
Fear listens to no voice but its own, while you —
You understand the secret language of the night
whispering your name.

Listen...
You belong to that conversation
as you belong to your life.

VISITOR

I AM A VISITOR HERE TO MY CHILDREN'S WORLD...
WHAT CAN I BRING?

I am the bow from which the arrow flies forth, where is
my home?

The tree nurtures the seed, but the seed listens to the wind
and follows that.

Releasing your children is relentless soul work – *learning
to let go of the ones you would die for.*

Afterward, only love remains.

The mother returns to herself after spending all in
birthing. *"Rest,"* she hears, *"Rest."*

Yet softly... quietly, the cat paws of her soul's body begin
to pad through the empty rooms, here and there sniff-
ing. Silently informing, *"There's more."*

The world has fragrance.

Eyes flicker open. She sighs and smiles, witness to the shape of her own breath in the chill morning air.

COMPASSION

COMPASSION IS THE COLOR OF TURQUOISE,
SMOOTH AND ROUND.

When you're ready, start close in...
don't take the next step or the next.
Open your heart to see what is here for you
now.

Start close in to feel what the stillness has held for you
since the dawn of time,
the love patiently awaiting you
everywhere you turn.

You are the wide blue sky,
don't pretend it isn't true!
When the sky enters you and you enter the sky,
clouds will simply be clouds passing...
passing.

Inner and outer will appear as One,
breathing perfect life as *You*...
creating the world anew in
shades of turquoise.

MEETING THE GODDESS

WHEN YOU MEET THE GODDESS, SHE WILL NOT
BE WEARING FAIRY WINGS.

She will not be all goodness and light,
nor will she dance *'airs above the ground'*.
She is all Earth and Darkness.
She is Silence and Gravity.
Her breasts are heavy, her body fecund,
weighted and exuding power.

When you meet the Goddess, her bare feet will be
caked with mud, her eyes hooded,
her shoulders rounded with care.
She will size you up without a glance,
take you in her mouth to chew slowly on your smallness.

She holds death in one hand and birth in the other like
two gleaming orbs resting lightly in the smooth center of
each palm.

When you meet the Goddess, bring her flowers.
Bring her your honest heart,
and your soul full of longing.
Bring her your tears and the hidden heat of your desire.
In that meeting, let fall your
garments stitched of past or future.
Stand naked before your mother,
allowing the mystery to blow away
all you once thought you were.

Sink your knees into wet earth
to be held in her embrace.
And when you are finally emptied,
breezes breathing through your bones,
she will at last turn her gaze to yours,
seeing the truth of who you are.

Crumble softly into her steadiness,
her strong arms and honest touch.
Die to be born again, to feel loved
as you were never loved by any mortal
here on earth.

WILD

THE WORLD IS WILD WITH TOOTH AND CLAW, AND SOFT
FEATHERY FUR.

The world is wild with curving thorn,
fragrant rose, surging waves and
glowing orange horizons.

Outside your window the hawk silently glides.
Over your roof, crackling blue lightning
electrifies the air.
Just beside your door, a fox listens intently,
poised to snatch its supper.

The world is more terrifying than your deepest fear,
more exquisite than imagination can conjure.

It is alive with wild creatures everywhere going about their business at all hours of day and night while you sleep without a care.

You must expect the unexpected, and
forget everything you thought you knew.
Give attention to the greater story
happening all around you.

It is an unfolding, unceasing and wordless spectacle which does
not wait for permission,
a command performance of primal deities appearing and disap-
pearing right before your eyes.

The world is free with fierce life unquenchable,
unstoppable...

I am wild too,
I have claws to grab and teeth to bite.
My eyes can be soft,
My hands open or shut tight.

FALLING OFF THE MOON

SHE SAID, *"HE FELL OFF THE MOON"* THE DAY HE
DIED, AND FELT SO SAD...

Those words imparted to innocents who called their
moon *"Charley's moon."*

Little ones who only knew he was gone but didn't under-
stand why.

Their child's eyes seeking the moon's round face as a way
of being with him, who had once gazed also into the
night sky.

She understood that the moon's cycle of waxing and
waning in reflected stellar beauty mirrored the bright
Giver of Life.

And perhaps found comfort that, much like her own
heart, the moon owned a dark side which did not face
the star it reflected yet belonged to itself all the same.

Now faced with the sudden finality of loss and remembering her ancient kinship with death, she uttered a silent prayer... asking how love and grief could heal the night-dark shadows of a human heart.

LENORE

When the door between worlds opens, the wheels of an ancient mystery begin to loosen and turn. Unseen hands are coming to lift the veil at the appointed hour.

Unknowing, we are their counterparts, sitting bedside with our beloved.

How does one leave her earthly body which housed such a gentle musical soul? A masterful composition of time measures the departure, and we learn to count each breath even while accepting the inevitable final surrender.

I wonder, does she see her own mother waiting for her? Does she remember the salty air of their beloved Cape May summers, her spirit already turned towards the new land and feeling the same childlike wonder?

We hold her hands long into the night while the world sleeps and dreams.

In my mind, I see the storied home of her childhood, her small body drifting down cool corridors barefooted in a white night shift which floats as she moves. Clear hazel eyes both innocent and wise seem to know that someone or something is coming soon.

Eyes which watch through shadowy nighttime windows, and gaze with an indefinable calm while a current of air ruffles curtains and the alchemy of night breezes counts her breaths.

We hold midnight vigil until the invisible angels arrive.

Suddenly, eyes opening, she mouths something first to my sister and then to me... communicating her whispered love. It takes everything she has. We strain to make out the words, feeling the final moment arriving.

In the silence which follows, a parting gift of peace fills and softens the space her soul once occupied. She has gone beyond, welcomed by unseen others who love her too, while we linger in our farewell, not ready to say goodbye.

DIFFERENT

I IMAGINED WE WERE SO DIFFERENT — SHE AND I.

Her east coast conservative upbringing and my sixties
generation values seemed light years apart.

We didn't hang out together the way some of my friends
did with their moms, cooking together or making
crafty things. We didn't chat on the phone much.

She loved my children and on that we agreed. Mothering
my own babies gave us common ground.

She was intellectual, reserved, musical and mystical. She
admired her psychic friend Eleanor and read Edgar
Cayce books. She adored my dad completely. She
played her Steinway with a passion not displayed for
any other pursuit.

I rode horses, backpacked, played guitar and sang, listened to rock and roll and experimented with sex secretly. Not surprisingly, I was pregnant at 16. A wild child by my mother's standards until marriage made me respectable.

We grew up in two different worlds, she and I. But when dad died and I became mom's lifeline, those differences didn't matter. Compassion and empathy did the work of dissolving any illusion that we really were separate.

When I sat with her in the hospice room, it washed over me how alike we really were. How dearly we held our family, our spirituality and music so close to heart. We both felt the same delight in growing roses, and the same peace in believing that the great mystery could indeed be trusted.

If two roads diverged in a yellow wood and I took the one less traveled, then the end of my mother's journey brought me full circle back to where we started... with an unexpected gift. Like putting a magic pebble in my pocket, her departing spirit granted me a superpower: the power to create my life as an expression of greater freedom and joy.

Every significant, lasting personal change in my life occurred for me after she left. Looking back, I now see this as my mother's parting gift to her middle daughter: the courage to start over and the grace to choose again.

MORE LIKE A TREE

I AM MORE LIKE A TREE THAN A LEAF.
I witness their drift and fall while
standing rooted, deeply watching,
holding time like holy breath.
Present to a life surging unseen from soil to cell,
alchemy moving upwards towards eternal sun,
bowing to the rhythmic truth of cycles and seasons.

I am more like a tree than a flower.
I revel in the flower's fragrant intoxication enticing honeybees in
the sharing of passing sweetness.
In the blooming season, I stand rejoicing in meadow warmth, as
family does, gathering the goodness of
smiles and laughter.
Creatures of the forest silently visit my home, bringing
an innocence which calls to my own.

I am more like a tree than the smooth flowing stream, though my
love catches her water as she sparkles, and my roots seek out her
coolness.
She and I have grown together and combined our wisdom.

She flows on and on, her destination the sea,
while I remain shaded, rooted and anchoring the sacred in place.
We are lovers forever entwined,
Two as One.

I know how to be a tree, to root down into one place.
My knowing bends in the wind
or spreads in the sun.
I know how to be a tree providing shade, respite and refuge to the
ones who have need of me.

Yes, I am most like a tree growing in the forest of
days and nights, transmitting memory through my skin.
My upward reach a bridge connecting
earth and sky, while
my roots converse unseen with
Silence, Mystery and Truth.

WHO WE ARE

A LILY IS NOT A ROSE, NOR IS THE ROSE AN IRIS.

The Hummingbird does not fly with the wings of Eagle,
nor does Robin sing with the voice of Raven.

We are who we are.

Don't waste any more precious time comparing yourself
to others!

Be who you came to be, and give what you came to give
before you leave this place.

ON SEEING

YOU SEE PHOTOS OF ME AS A YOUNG CHILD, INNOCENT AND CURIOUS. Wide dark eyes still open and shining from the radiant realm that sent me. Skin smooth and untouched by time, baby fat puckering knees and elbows.
Adorable, but...

This is not who I am.

See me vibrant in my youth, long hair flowing, bright with promise, sweet and unwritten. Idealistic, naïve, ready for anything and eager to feel everything.
Longing for the freedom of being launched by the rocket fuel of my own imagination.

This is not who I am.

See me with babes nestled in my arms, fierce earth mother instinct flowing through my body, protecting my young and digging deeper to find new strength.
Loving stubbornly while surrendering to the years of requests and demands. The responsibilities of mother and teacher defining my shape in the world...

This is not who I am.

Now see me with new wrinkles, a face well-traveled. A voice that has sung many songs. A heart cracked open and mended with Elmer's. Hair thinning and fading, body slowing, and eyes filled with memory.
A multitude of evolutions, revolutions and reincarnations all in one tired body. Tucked away in my small corner of the world feeling quiet and grateful.

This is not who I am.

See me as I cared for my parents, sad and surprised at their frailty. Wondering how to be that good daughter with a deeper under-standing of forgiveness, compassion and care. Grieving the godlike parents who gave me everything. Loving in a new way the gentle souls that loved me so well.

This is not who I am.

You may think you know who I am, but you cannot know that. Even I, with my intimate knowledge of self, am still uncovering my soul's structure - the bones of my reason for being.

You cannot see me truly in the old way of seeing,
so let your gaze go unfocused.
Turn on peripheral vision and watch it expand to
sense the subtle world of vibration and frequency.

Go past the body and into the field.

Then, open the window in your chest to see the one who stands
before you, inhaling my soul's fragrance.
Say hello from there.

LOVE AND BE LOVED

Time passes...
and we arrive and depart
according to
our own
hour.

I am here to love and
be loved,
I am here to love
and be loved.

Time passes and the faces around me change for
life is a moving river, yet
time passes and
I am still here.

I am here to love and be loved
I am here to love and be
I am here to love
I am here
I am.

PRAYER FOR THE BROKEN

MOTHER FATHER GOD, HELP ME TODAY TO BE THE
STILLNESS OF THE FALLOW FIELD BEFORE THE FIRST
SEEDING.

Help me to sit deeply in emptiness, in groundlessness,
not grabbing onto anything or anyone.

Allow me to be in the not knowing, to float in mystery without
raising my eyes to seek a familiar shore.

Help me today to stay crumbled, to be an awareness inside the
devastation, to be clay before ever the potter's hand is felt.

Let me be a flame, ever dancing and burning away all that is non-
essential in me.

Let me remain standing on my own ground of being
without shame or fear.

Help me to be canvas resting before the artist's brush,
to be that spaciousness which lives before thought births itself.

Show me how to live in this body within this life,
to feel this sorrow and this tenderness without moving to make it
mean anything.

Show me how to die well and truly, to die so that I may live,
but to die nonetheless without attachment to outcome.

Mother Father God, help me today to be the dark silence before
dawn, the in-breath before crying out, a container for emptiness
and the pure Awareness which lives inside That.

Amen.

ON VULNERABILITY

OPEN YOUR VOICE.

Step past your first fear to allow breath and sound. Come out little one, *you are safe here.*

Return from your long absence and come home.

There is a moment of decision before voice utters sound, but silence only offers the illusion of safety.

Step into the brightly lit moment when eyes look up at you, ready to receive your song.

Dig deeply for the courage to allow yourself to be seen and heard.

The coin of vulnerability that frightens you is also your strength.

Your tender willingness opens the inner sanctum and invites the soul to return to its true home.

Do you want to touch the truth now?

Make a sound. Step out of sweet silence. Open your
precious voice!

Our hearts are waiting to receive the first tremulous note,
bearing witness to your voice joining all the other
angels singing for every sunrise on earth.

PRAYER FOR PEACE

WHATEVER BRINGS LOVE, WHATEVER BRINGS
   LIGHT,

Whatever allows healing – let it be done.
Whatever shares joy, whatever gives comfort,
Whatever sparks forgiveness – let it be done.

May all my relationships proclaim love,
May all my relationships demonstrate peace,
May all my relationships lift the world higher.

Let it be done, let it be done.
Not my will but Thine be done.
I am grateful, I am thankful,
I am open and surrendered.

Let me be an instrument of Thy peace
Let it be done, let it be.
May Your voice sing forever in me.

Amen.

HOW TO WRITE A POEM

THE PRACTICE OF NOTICING IS AT THE CENTER OF
EVERYTHING. It finds you when you are completely still – when
the boat that is you drifts into calm waters and slows down to the
pace of silence.

When you stop to deeply listen, the gods reveal a universe made of
cosmic nuance.

Poems, songs, melodies, inspired words are all first felt as embodi-
ment. The divine whispers into your listening when your entire
being becomes a receptor and every cell is an ear.

The soft breeze caressing your skin seeks and finds its home in the
heart, speaking softly in the sensual language of melody, taste, or
scent. This subtle embodiment arriving unannounced is some-
times a sound, sometimes a word or phrase, and always a feeling.

Fragrance when cultivated and honored makes its home in you as
a seed – a divine seed attracting all that is true to its cosmic DNA:
colors, textures, tones, images, words that carry its essence and
sounds that resonate with its vibrational frequency.

Hindu tradition tells us that magical beings called Gandharvas give songs to those who hear them – melodies carried by the air and transmitted through the skin. To one who practices listening with devotion, these transmissions have the scent of breezes from far-off lands… winds that have traveled across miles of ocean to greet you where you live and meet you in your house of belonging.

With awareness – every breath, every turn of the wheel, and each human experience becomes a way to expand beyond the self. Our attention makes us a vehicle for the divine and a gateway for truth and beauty to enter the world.

In this conscious allowing, we offer our voices not to sing, but to be sung; our words not to be written by us but through us. Our listening in each moment creates within us a light – a beacon of welcome and a home for the great song to gather us up into bands of angels singing for a new world.

So…if your heart of hearts longs to create – start by listening. Notice your surroundings and ask, "What is here?" Pay attention to how you feel and to what is moving through you. *What is that feeling?*

Does it speak to you?

Like honey, your own readiness and willingness will attract and capture the transmission. But be mindful, for the Muse doesn't linger! When she visits, offer her wine and a seat at the table. A meal is already being prepared and filling your house with delicious aromas.

Sit, sit… feast on your life… feast on your life.

WAITING FOR RAIN

THERE'S A FEELING RIGHT BEFORE IT RAINS when
   clouds blanket the light and suddenly the whole
   world goes still.

Rain is coming.

Slowly, like a procession of the elements wind begins
   speaking to trees, orchestrating breezes that playfully
   lift with delicate airy fingers, directing an eager
   cadence of leaves to make their secret sound.

Rain is coming.

Heralded by the first translucent droplets too small to
   sound but holding memory and promise, misty hands
   caress my cheek lightly with their cool touch and
   delight my child's heart with the scent of something
   completely new.

Fat drops ride in on gusts of air while the chorus of leaves
   shout, *Open! Open!* to the gathering sky gods.

Rain is here!

Rhythmic and rising in crescendo, softening then rising
again, waves of moisture rejoice in the sudden
freedom of release.

Rain!

Falling in a symphony of fullness, trees and earth
sounding with wind fueling the growing chorus and
all the earth drinking from the sky in grateful gulps.

Rain kissing the ground once again with unconditional
blessing, falling on saint and sinner alike before gently
lifting her skirts to make a graceful exit.

We follow her with our eyes, our innocence restored, our
souls filled with wonder.

ABOUT THE AUTHOR

ABOUT THE AUTHOR
A voracious reader since childhood, Devavani is a gifted creator, teacher and musician who loves using her voice to inspire others through writing, poetry and song. She discovered libraries as a young girl and was an avid reader and writer at an early age. Her love of travel, nature and adventure led her to live on the tiny island of Guam with wife Donna and little dog Scout, where she grows bananas and sings with a beautiful community of friends.

Devavani likes hearing from her readers and encourages people to email her at: devavani333@gmail.com. ***Devavani Vocal Arts*** offers classes online and in person for anyone desiring to explore their own creative voice in writing, singing, voice yoga or the art of spoken word.

For more information about current offerings, please visit **https://DevavaniVocalArts.com**

GRATITUDES

No one walks their path alone and I wish to thank those friends and family who have healed me, loved me, sang with me, made me laugh and held sacred my desire to express myself creatively:

Rev. Dr. Kathy Hearn for her compassionate spiritual nurturing and friendship, Sheri Mozdir for lifelong friendship and wise counsel, Supriya Ishaya for co-creating women's retreats with me and flying to Kauai to officiate our wedding vows, Wendy Gatto for her bottomless ability to witness my grief with a light and tender heart, Lisa Pridmore who sold me her magical desert home when I needed it, Pamela Underwood for her women's body-writing weekends, Silvia Nakkach for *Yoga of the Voice* and the life-giving raga sangeet class that kept my head above water during the pandemic, Jan Rowden, Neika Whittemore and Fenella Speece for asking me to write this book and sending seed money, Rev. Kevin Bucy & the many friends and fellow musicians at Universal Spirit Center who created heart-opening music with me week after week, Peggy Lebo and Teri Wilder who lifted me with their love, laughter and musical partnership, Annette Ridenour and Myron Stam who believed in me and gave generously of their love, time and talent, my daughters Jessica and Rosie who continue to inspire me with their passion, love and strength, my loving sisters Laura and Marni who never let go of me, Beth Barany who appeared in my life just in time to help me birth this book, and last but never least, my extraordinary wife Donna Lawrence, whose greatest dream for me is to live with uncompromising joy and freedom.

If I did not name everyone, it is only because I have been so blessed by so many. Please know that I am deeply and forever thankful to all the friends, family, and beloved pets who lent their love and strength to my journey.